Collins

WEATHER

FASCINATING FACTS

Published by Collins
An imprint of HarperCollins Publishers
Westerhill Road
Bishopbriggs
Glasgow G64 2QT
www.harpercollins.co.uk

First published 2016

A catalogue record for this book is available from the British Library

ISBN 978-0-00-816921-3

10 9 8 7 6 5 4 3 2 1

Printed in China by R R Donnelley APS Co Ltd.

Collins Bartholomew, the UK's leading independent geographical information supplier, can provide a digital, custom, and premium mapping service to a variety of markets.
For further information:
Tel: +44 (0)208 307 4515
e-mail: collinsbartholomew@harpercollins.co.uk
Visit our website at: www.collins.co.uk   www.collinsbartholomew.com

If you would like to comment on any aspect of this book, please contact us at the above address or online.
e-mail: collinsmaps@harpercollins.co.uk

MIX
Paper from
responsible sources
FSC™ C007454

www.fsc.org

FSC™ is a non-profit international organisation established to promote the responsible management of the world's forests. Products carrying the FSC label are independently certified to assure consumers that they come from forests that are managed to meet the social, economic and ecological needs of present and future generations, and other controlled sources.

Find out more about HarperCollins and the environment at
www.harpercollins.co.uk/green

Contents

Wonderful weather

Weather affects us all. It is the ever-changing conditions in the air around us. In some places around the world the weather hardly changes from day to day. But in other places the weather is a daily topic of conversation because no two days are ever the same.

What is it all about?

This book aims to explore lots of fascinating facts all about the weather. It will try to answer some questions you may have, for example, why does it rain? How is snow formed? What are the wildest storms? Where are the hottest places? How is weather measured? What is climate change and how might that affect our weather?

A weather poem

Whether the weather be fine
or whether the weather be not,
Whether the weather is cold
or whether the weather is hot,
We'll weather the weather,
Whatever the weather,
Whether we like it or not!

Anon

What is weather?

Atmosphere

The atmosphere is like a blanket surrounding the Earth. It gives us the air we breathe, and protects us from extreme temperatures. The atmosphere provides just the right conditions for life on our planet. Without an atmosphere there would be no weather.

What is the atmosphere made of?

It is made up of 78% nitrogen gas, 21% oxygen, tiny amounts of argon gas and water in the form of vapour, droplets, and crystals. It also contains some particles of dust, soot, pollen, and salt from the oceans.

Unlike Earth, the Moon has no atmosphere at all. It has no sky and no weather. Astronauts who walked on the Moon looked out into the blackness of space. Like in this picture, they saw the blues and greens of the oceans and landmasses on Earth and white cloud systems in its atmosphere.

Did you know?

Jet planes fly at the top of the troposphere to avoid bad weather.

Layers of the atmosphere

Our atmosphere is made up of different layers. The **troposphere** is the layer closest to the ground and it is the changes within this layer which cause our weather. Above this is the **stratosphere**. The **ozone** layer protects us from the Sun's harmful rays. The other layers that make up the atmosphere are the **mesosphere**, the **thermosphere**, and the **exosphere**.

This diagram clearly shows the layers of the atmosphere.
······························▶

Jet streams

Weather forecasters often talk about our weather being affected by jet streams. These are high winds in the top part of the stratosphere which move high and low pressure systems around over large areas. The weather systems that are carried by jet streams have a big impact on the weather around the globe.

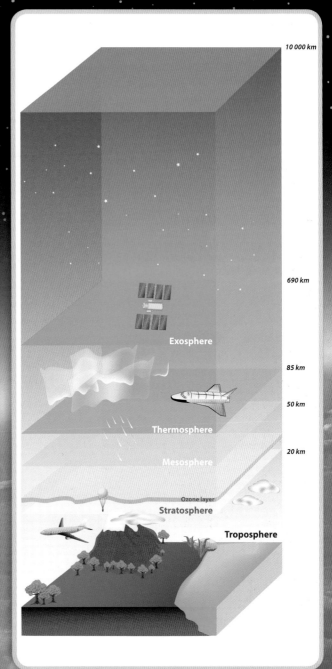

10 000 km

690 km

Exosphere

85 km

50 km

Thermosphere

20 km

Mesosphere

Ozone layer
Stratosphere

Troposphere

9

Clouds

Clouds are formed by moisture that has been heated up to form gas and which has then gone into the air. When the air is cold enough the gas turns back into moisture, which attaches to tiny dust particles to form clouds. Clouds are given different names based on their height and shape.

Cumulus clouds

Cumulus clouds are the most common type of clouds. They are mainly fluffy and white like balls of cotton wool. When they grow bigger they often have flat bases which sit about 1 km from the ground. Clouds with tops like cauliflower heads are called **cumulus congestus**. On hot days some cumulus clouds may grow upwards into huge thunderclouds called **cumulonimbus**.

Water turns to steam when boiled in a kettle. When the steam meets the cooler air, it condenses and we can see it. This is similar to how clouds are formed.

Cumulus congestus

Stratus clouds

Bands or layers of cloud are given the name **stratus**. **Cirrostratus** is a very high-up band of thin cloud containing ice crystals. **Altostratus** forms a thin grey sheet of cloud cover which the Sun can sometimes hazily shine through. **Nimbostratus** is a thicker blanket of cloud with rain in it. **Stratocumulus** is more dark and rounded.

A stratus cloud in a blue sky.

Fog is stratus cloud that has formed at or come down to ground level.

Cirrus clouds

Cirrus clouds are very thin and wispy high-level clouds made of ice crystals. Sometimes winds blow through them and produce streamers known as 'mares' tails' because they look similar to horses' tails.

Cirrus clouds take their name from the Latin word 'cirrus', meaning a curling lock of hair.

Different types of clouds

The various types of cloud can be found at different heights above the ground – some clouds are found at low levels and some are seen high in the sky.

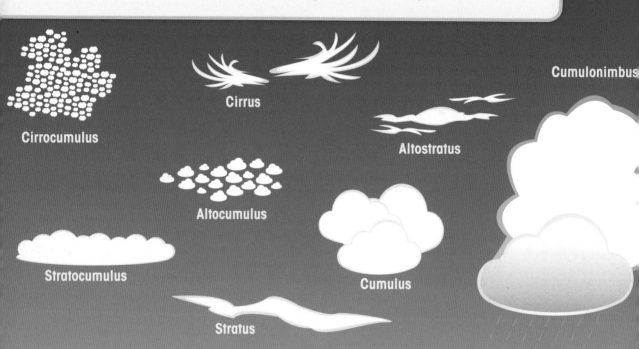

Cirrocumulus

Cirrus

Cumulonimbus

Altostratus

Altocumulus

Stratocumulus

Cumulus

Stratus

Cloud type	Height above ground
stratus stratocumulus cumulus	1800 metres (6000 feet) or lower
altocumulus altostratus	1800 metres to 6000 metres (6000 feet to 20 000 feet)
cirrocumulus cirrus	5500 metres (18 000 feet) and higher
cumulonimbus	Occur anywhere between 0 metres and 15 000 metres (50 000 feet)

Pictures in the clouds

Some people call themselves 'cloud spotters' and they enjoy observing and taking photographs of all shapes and sizes of clouds.

What do you see in the clouds?

Rain

Some clouds have ice crystals and snowflakes in them but by the time they reach the lower layers of the atmosphere, these fall as rain. In warmer areas, rain falls when water droplets in clouds join together. Rain-bearing clouds often look grey and dark.

Facts about rain

Another name for rain is **precipitation**. Rain usually falls at a speed of between 11 and 29 kilmoetres per hour but can fall faster if the wind is blowing. Sometimes rain falls as light drizzle, other times it is a downpour. A long spell of rain is called 'persistent rain'. Rain can sometimes contain dirt, dust, insects, grass, or even chemicals.

This diagram shows the **water cycle** on Earth. Moisture evaporates from the oceans and forms clouds. As clouds move upwards into cooler areas, moisture condenses into droplets which attach to dust particles. When clouds get too heavy, rain falls to the ground and the water returns to the oceans. This whole process then repeats itself.

The water cycle

1. Heat from the sun causes water to evaporate.

2. The water vapour rises, cools and creates clouds.

3. The clouds build up and shed water as rain.

4. The rain water flows downhill and back to the sea.

Sea level

Rainbows

A rainbow is an arc of colour bands in the sky. Rainbows occur when there is sun shining through rain. A rainbow will form opposite the Sun. Raindrops split up the white light from the Sun into all the colours of the spectrum. These colours are red, orange, yellow, green, blue, indigo, and violet. Many people use rhymes to remember the order of colours in a rainbow.

Make your own rainbow

Try making your own rainbow by placing a glass of water or an angled clear plastic ruler above a sheet of white paper. Place the glass near direct sunlight to make a beam of white light. Light passing through the glass or ruler will be split up into its rainbow colours.

Like this example in Thailand, a sun halo is caused by light being bent through high-level ice crystals in very thin cirrus clouds.

Sunshine

We get light and heat from our star, the Sun. The Earth is one of eight planets that move around the Sun. The Sun gives off tremendous amounts of heat, radiation, and light. It has a huge effect on the weather on Earth.

The Sun's energy

Not all of the sun's energy reaches the Earth. The atmosphere soaks up 19% of it and 30% of its energy is reflected back into space by clouds or the Earth's surface. Only 51% of the Sun's energy is absorbed by the Earth's surface.

This is the surface of the Sun.

Some of the Sun's energy is reflected back out into space.

16

Recording sunshine

Meteorologists traditionally used a Campbell-Stokes recorder to measure hourly or daily sunshine. This is a solid glass ball which is used to focus the Sun's rays and burn a trace onto a specially-made sunshine recorder card. It records bright sunshine in either hourly or daily totals.

A Campbell–Stokes recorder is named after its inventor, John Campbell, and the man who adapted it, George Stokes.

Why is the sky blue?

Light that comes from the Sun is white. White is made up of all the colours of the spectrum. But the colours all have different **wavelengths**. Blue has the shortest wavelength and so gets scattered by the atmosphere all around the sky. This makes the sky look blue during the day. Longer wavelength colours such as red and orange pass straight through the air.

Why are sunsets red?

Sunsets or sunrises often give yellow, orange, and red skies. This is because the Sun is low down and its light has to go through thicker layers of atmosphere. This allows colours that have longer wavelengths, such as red and orange, to be seen.

Wind

Wind is made by the air moving. If you wave your hand in front of your face you will cause a slight breeze. Winds cause clouds to move and whole weather systems to shift from one place to another.

What makes the air move?

Warm air rises up. The Sun's rays heat up the Earth over the **equator** and this warm air rises up and then cools. The spin of the Earth makes the air move either north or south at a height of about 7 to 10 km above the Earth. Then the air falls back to the ground and heads back to the Equator.

Did you know?

Many plants use wind to scatter their seeds, like this dandelion.

Winds that are north and south of the Equator are called **trade winds**. Winds that blow from west to east are called the **westerlies**.

60°
Westerlies
30°
Trade winds
0°
Trade winds
30°
Westerlies
60°

Arctic and polar continental winds

In winter, Arctic and polar continental winds bring sunny, clear, and dry but cold weather. However in summer they bring cold and showery weather. Wind which comes over polar seas brings cold and heavy showers of rain and snow.

↑ Wind and clouds over frozen snow in Lapland.

Tropical continental winds

These winds come from the land north and south of the equator. They hold dry, warm air. Sometimes dust from areas such as the Sahara Desert in North Africa can be blown northwards across Europe. Occasionally car owners in the south of Britain find their cars covered in red desert dust!

↑ Sometimes red dust from the Sahara Desert will be carried by the wind to Europe.

Tropical maritime winds

Tropical maritime winds form over the oceans in the tropics and bring fine, mainly warm weather. But if they do come from an area where low pressure has caused storms and rain, they will carry damp wet weather to places.

Snow

When it is cold enough, the moisture in clouds turns into ice crystals. These crystals can grow in size because either more moisture freezes onto them or they bump together and join up. If it is cold enough at ground level, these crystals fall as snowflakes.

The highest mountain in Africa is often covered in snow.
...............................➤

Snowflakes

Seen under a microscope, snowflakes are amazing structures. Many are hexagonal shapes, the most common one being a six-pointed star shape. Other shapes are columns and needles. Some snowflakes are made of six branches connecting into the centre – these are called **dendrites**. **Plates** are snowflakes that have not quite been able to form a star. No two snowflakes are the same.

Did you know?

Many countries have hundreds of words for different kinds of snow.

Where do you get snow?

Snow needs low temperatures and moisture to form. Therefore it is found at places at higher **latitudes** such as nearer the North and South Poles and at high **altitudes** such as at the top of mountains. Florida has lots of moisture in the air but is usually too warm for snow. Antarctica is the coldest continent but it is also the driest. There is an area called 'Dry Valleys' in Antarctica which actually gets no snow.

Different types of snow

A mixture of snow and rain is called sleet. Snow that is very dry is called powder snow. Powder snow is most likely to cause **avalanches**. Skiers call powder snow which has been pressed down 'crud'. They call snow that has melted and then frozen again 'crust'. Slush is when snow is melting and is soft and watery.

A woman skiing in powder snow in the mountains – as she turns she causes a small avalanche.

21

Ice and glaciers

Ice is formed by water freezing or snow being pressed down when temperatures are below 0° Celsius. A very large area of ice in the mountains is called a **glacier**.

This waterfall has frozen.

Why do we put salt on paths?

Putting salt on ice lowers its melting point and so helps it thaw out quicker. That is why we spread grit, or rock salt, on the roads in winter when it gets really cold.

Try out this experiment. Pour water into a plastic tub. Place some small plastic figures or models in the water. Leave in a freezer overnight.

Take the tub out and sprinkle some salt over one of the figures. Now leave them both to thaw at room temperature and watch what happens.

This game of curling is taking place on a frozen Lake of Menteith in Scotland, UK in January 2010.

Glaciers

When snow falls year after year in the same place it gets pressed down and forms ice, called a glacier. This ice gets so thick and heavy that it can start to move very slowly. At present 10% of Earth's land area is covered in ice and glaciers. Some glaciers are the size of football pitches, others can be hundreds of kilometres long.

Global climate records

Scientists drill out samples of ice which hold clues to Earth's climate in the past. Trapped air bubbles and vegetation show what past air temperatures would have been. In the past 750 000 years there have been eight Ice Ages with warmer periods in between. Evidence shows that right now the world's glaciers and ice sheets are melting at a much faster than normal rate, believed to be due to global warming.

The Perito Moreno Glacier is a glacier in the Los Glaciares National Park in Argentina. It is one of the most important tourist attractions in this part of Argentina.

Glaciers are mainly found in mountainous or polar regions. Huge glaciers and ice shelves can be found in Antarctica.

Understanding weather

Seasons

Seasons are different times of the year which feature certain weather conditions, temperatures, and lengths of daylight.

Earth takes 365 days a year to go around the Sun. Different places get varying amounts of sunlight because of the Earth's tilt.

summer

spring

autumn

Why do we get seasons?

Our planet spins on an axis as it travels around the Sun. But because this axis is tilted, there are times in the year when parts of Earth get more or less sunlight and heat than at other times. For example, the northern half of the Earth is tilted towards the Sun when the southern half is tilted away from the Sun.

Seasons across the world

The year is divided into seasons. The length of each season can vary depending on how far a place is from the Equator. These dials show the pattern of seasons in the northern hemisphere.

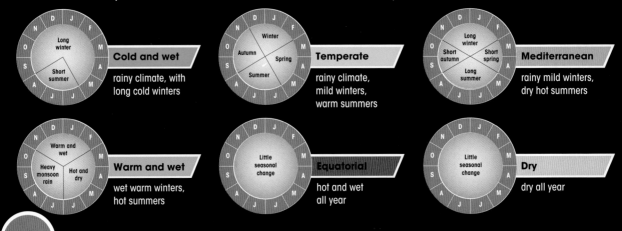

Cold and wet
rainy climate, with long cold winters

Long winter / Short summer

Temperate
rainy climate, mild winters, warm summers

Winter / Autumn / Spring / Summer

Mediterranean
rainy mild winters, dry hot summers

Long winter / Short autumn / Short spring / Long summer

Warm and wet
wet warm winters, hot summers

Warm and wet / Heavy monsoon rain / Hot and dry

Equatorial
hot and wet all year

Little seasonal change

Dry
dry all year

Little seasonal change

The four seasons

Temperate areas have four main seasons: spring, summer, autumn, and winter. Meteorologists give set months for each season in the northern hemisphere:

Spring: March 1st – May 31st
Summer: June 1st – August 31st
Autumn: September 1st – November 30th
Winter: December 1st – February 28th/29th

Winter is the coldest season and has the shortest days. Days can be cold, crisp, and clear with ice and frost, or rainy and snowy. In spring the days get longer and warmer. Summer is the time when many people take holidays to make the most of the long days and hot sunshine, although some places can still be rainy in summer. Autumn is cooler and darker and many trees put on a show of dazzling yellows, reds, oranges, and browns before the leaves fall off. In North America, autumn is known as the 'fall'.

A December snowman in North America.

In the southern hemisphere the seasons are the complete opposite to those in the northern hemisphere.

A December 'snowman' in Australia.

Measuring rainfall

Rain is collected in rain gauges and is measured either in centimetres and millimetres or in inches.

Rain gauges are also called **udometers**, **pluviometers**, or **ombrometers**. Traditional gauges are containers which are shaped like a cylinder or a funnel.

It is important for meteorologists to keep good rainfall records. They need to keep a check on the different amounts of rainfall from place to place and over different periods of time. They can use measurements to help them understand weather patterns better.

A male ruby-throated hummingbird sitting on a rain gauge.
.........................➤

Make your own rain gauge

You will need
- an empty plastic bottle without its cap on (2 litre size is best)
- scissors
- clear sticky tape
- a ruler
- a strip of paper, 20 cm x 5 cm
- a pencil

Instructions
Cut the plastic bottle around where the bottle starts to curve at the top.

Then turn the top part upside down and place it inside the bottom part, fixing it in place with sticky tape.

Draw on a scale in centimetres along the strip of paper and stick this up the side of the bottle with zero at the very bottom.

Cover the paper strip completely with clear sticky tape to keep it waterproof.

Siting the rain gauge
Now find an open site to put your gauge. You may want to dig a hole for it and put it in so that half of it is sticking out the hole. This will stop it blowing away.

Try and check your rain gauge at the same time every day and keep a record of the rainfall. You could make a graph of the results.

Temperature is measured using units called degrees Centigrade or Celsius (shortened to °C). An older unit of measurement that some people still use is degrees Fahrenheit (°F).

Thermometers are used to measure temperatures. They work by having a liquid (often liquid mercury) inside them which expands when heated and shrinks when cool.

This thermometer measures temperature in both Celsius and Fahrenheit.

On the thermometer below the blue colour shows freezing temperatures. If the needle points below zero there will be frost and ice outside as water freezes at 0 °C.

At 20 °C the weather is pleasantly warm, 30 °C is hot, and 40 °C is uncomfortably hot for many people.

Galileo thermometer

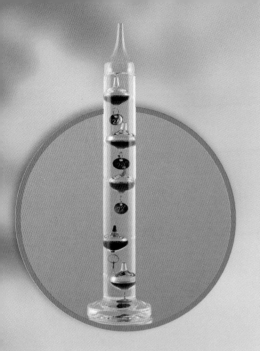

In the 17th century a scientist called Galileo noticed that liquid in a glass container expanded or shrank depending on how hot or cold the atmosphere was. His observation led to the invention of the thermometer.

This is called a 'Galileo thermometer'. The weights float to the top according to how warm or cold the liquid gets.

Make your own thermometer

You will need
- an empty plastic water bottle (about 500 ml)
- some surgical spirit
- a clear plastic drinking straw
- food colouring
- a piece of Blu-Tack®

Instructions
Fill the bottle with a mixture of water and surgical spirit until it is one quarter full. Add in some food colouring. Put the plastic straw into the liquid and attach it at the top of the bottle with the Blu-Tack®. The straw should not touch the bottom of the bottle or be able to move. Also make sure the straw sticks out the top of the Blu-Tack® but the rest of the bottle top is airtight.

Now cup your hands around the bottom of the bottle. Watch how the coloured liquid rises up through the straw.

Measuring wind

Wind vanes or wind socks have long been used to measure the direction and strength of the wind. **Anemometers** have been used to measure wind speed. Nowadays digital instruments can measure both.

The Beaufort Scale

In 1805 a British naval officer called Francis Beaufort invented a scale based on what had been observed on land and at sea that would help the Royal Navy record wind conditions. The scale goes from 1 (a calm flat sea) all the way to 12 (hurricane conditions). In between, the scale ranges from breezes to gales depending on the size of waves, their white crests, and the amount of spray in the air. Radio shipping forecasts still use terms from this scale.

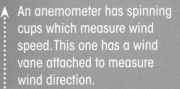

An anemometer has spinning cups which measure wind speed. This one has a wind vane attached to measure wind direction.

Wind socks can be seen at airports showing quickly and clearly the wind direction and strength.

Make a flower pot wind vane

You will need
- a pencil with an eraser on the end
- a pin
- a plastic straw
- the lid of a margarine tub
- scissors
- a small flower pot filled with soil
- 4 wooden clothes pegs
- a compass

Instructions
First use the pencil to mark the top of the pegs, one with N, another E, next S, and lastly W. Peg these markers around the edge of the flower pot.

Now cut two triangles, one bigger than the other, out of the plastic lid of a margarine tub. Cut a slit at each end of the straw and slide the triangles in at each end. The smaller one should point outwards and the larger one should point inwards towards the smaller one.

Push the pin down through the middle of the straw and then down into the pencil eraser. Finally push the pencil point a few centimetres into the flower pot.

Siting the wind vane
Take your wind vane outside and place it on a flat even surface like the top of a wall, a bench, or even a bird table. Use a compass to line up the north peg on the pot with true north. When the wind blows, the wind vane should spin round to show the direction of the wind.

Measuring pressure

In 1643 Galileo's assistant, Evangelista Torricelli, discovered that the Earth's atmosphere had weight. This weight is called **atmospheric pressure**. It was found that changes in the weather were related to changes in pressure. This led to the invention of an instrument called the **barometer**.

Weather charts

Meteorologists 'join-the-dots' with atmospheric pressure to create weather charts. Pressure is measured in **millibars** (mb) or hectopascals (hPa) and points of equal pressure are joined up on maps to form lines called **isobars**. The result is something which looks like a contour map but instead of showing hills and valleys, it shows 'highs' and 'lows' of pressure.

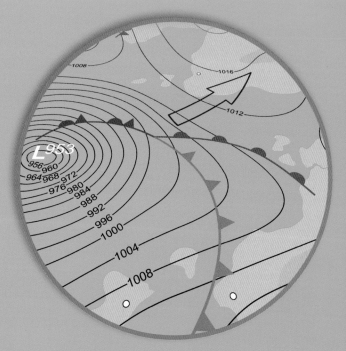

Fronts are lines drawn across isobars that show the edges of pressure systems. Triangles on them show cold fronts, semicircles show warm fronts and a mix shows where one front is meeting another.

Many people use a barometer to look for changes in the weather.

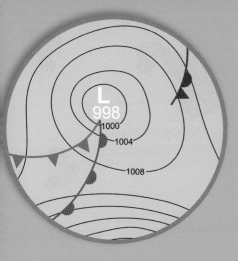

Reading isobars

Air pressure ranges between 890 mb (a **cyclone** or low pressure) to 1060 mb (an **anticyclone** or high pressure).

Sometimes the isobars form circles. Where the highest number is in a circle this marks a high pressure system, which is shown by the letter H. Usually high pressure areas bring dry, sunny weather.

Where the lowest number is in a circle this marks a low pressure system, which is shown by the letter L or sometimes T for **trough**. Low pressure brings wet and windy weather.

The closer the isobars are together, the windier it is.

Isobar maps are shown less these days as forecasters tend to show satellite photographs instead.

Weather stations

In 1873 there was a world meeting of meteorologists in Vienna, Austria. It was agreed that all countries would have the same type of weather station. This meant the equipment used by weather recorders and the way records were to be kept would be exactly the same. They also decided on special international weather codes.

Weather stations

All weather stations are placed outside to measure temperatures, amount of moisture in the air (humidity), rainfall, hours of sunlight, wind, and air pressure. A traditional weather station is a white box with slats in the sides. The box helps to protect the more delicate instruments.

In some parts of Europe you might see a **weather house** which is supposed to tell you what the weather is going to be like. In this weather house, when the woman is out, it is sunny, but when the man with the umbrella comes out, it is going to rain.

Weather stations in space

Some weather stations can be found in the satellites that orbit Earth. They can look at 'space weather', for example when particles shoot out from the Sun and enter Earth's atmosphere. These particles can create colourful light displays such as the **aurora borealis.** Some weather forecasts will tell you when you might expect to see an aurora display.

Aurora displays are known as **northern lights** or **southern lights** depending on whether they are near the North or South Pole.

Forecasting the weather

Meteorologists give short-term and long-term weather forecasts. Nowadays weather **satellites** give images and data which, when entered into a computer, make weather forecasts more accurate.

However the weather is very unpredictable and conditions can change very quickly.

Meteorologists can study satellite images to predict more accurately what the weather will be.

Forecasters may also use symbols on weather maps or on mobile phone apps. Forecasts are at our fingertips more now than ever before.

Did you know?

In Britain there is a well-known BBC forecast known as 'The Shipping Forecast' which gives forecasts for conditions at sea around the country.

Weather sayings

People have always watched the weather and there are some sayings that hold true to this day. For example:

'The north wind doth blow and we shall have snow.'

Indeed northerly winds do bring down cold Arctic air, which sometimes clashes with moister warm air and brings snow.

'When the wind is out of the east, 'tis never good for man nor beast.'

Winds which blow from Eastern Europe and Russia bring bitterly cold winds in winter.

Red skies

If there is a red sky in the northern hemisphere at dawn, this means the sun is shining low on rain clouds and so bad weather is probably coming in from the west.

However, if the sun is shining low on clouds at sunset, this could mean a wet front is moving east and better weather is coming in from the west.

> Red sky in the morning, shepherds' warning.
> Red sky at night, shepherds' delight.
>
> (Sometimes sailors replace shepherds in this saying.)

Written in the clouds

Clouds are often a good way of telling what the weather is going to be like.

Small cumulus clouds show fair weather but if they grow bigger, showers are forming. If they grow huge and dark, then wet weather is on its way.

Cirrus clouds are a sign that rain is coming since these clouds are formed ahead of warm fronts bringing moisture off the sea.

Streaky clouds like the markings on mackerel fish can indicate showery weather. An old saying is:

'Mackerel sky, mackerel sky,
Never long wet, never long dry.'

Extreme weather

Hurricanes

Hurricanes are massive tropical storms with heavy rain and winds ranging from 120 to 320 km/h (75 to 200 mph). They form over warm water and can grow to be 1000 km (600 miles) wide. If they hit land they cause coastal flooding and huge damage to buildings, vehicles, trees, and crops.

Why do they form?

Hurricanes begin as areas of low pressure over warm ocean water. As warm water heats up and evaporates, this is drawn upwards into cooler air. Wind blows air up and out above the storm causing yet more air to rise. As the storm picks up more energy it begins to spin and spiral, growing bigger and bigger.

Hurricanes move over the oceans at between 16 and 32 km/h (10 and 20 mph).

Hurricanes cause huge destruction if they hit land. Over the last two centuries more than 2 million people have died as a result of hurricanes.

Scientists use weather satellites to track the movement of hurricanes, such as this enormous hurricane over the Atlantic.

Hurricane Sandy destroyed homes in New York City in 2012.

Cyclones and typhoons

Hurricanes are called **typhoons** in the northwest Pacific near Japan. Where they occur in the south Pacific Ocean or Indian Ocean they are named **cyclones**. The term hurricane is used for the massive storms in the Atlantic Ocean that affect the eastern seaboard of the USA and the Caribbean islands.

Palm trees bend in the high winds of a cyclone.

The morning after Typhoon Yolanda hit Panay Island in the Philippines.

Why do hurricanes spin?

Hurricanes spin because the Earth's spinning creates a force which affects the winds. Winds in hurricanes north of the equator spin in an anticlockwise direction. Those that are south of the Equator spin in a clockwise direction.

Did you know?

Hurricanes are given names from six sets of lists in alphabetical order. If a hurricane causes a lot of damage, such as Hurricane Katrina in 2012, the name is not used again. Hurricane Katrina hit the US city of New Orleans. 1800 people were killed and there was huge damage to the city.

The aftermath of Hurricane Katrina in New Orleans

Tornadoes

A tornado is a fast swirling funnel of extremely high winds which touches the ground. It looks like a grey elephant trunk that sucks up whatever lies in its path like the hose of a vacuum cleaner.

Tornadoes form when low-down warm air meets high cold polar winds and there is a sudden and intense drop in pressure between one air mass and another.

Tornadoes occur mostly over dry plains and can happen on almost every continent. However, they are most common over the plains of southern USA, which have about 1000 tornadoes a year. Indeed there is an area called 'Tornado Valley', which runs through the states of Texas, Oklahoma, Kansas, Nebraska, and Dakota.

Europe occasionally gets smaller funnels that touch ground as tornadoes.

When a funnel touches water it creates what is known as a 'waterspout'.

Did you know?
In North America, tornadoes are also called twisters.

Make your own tornado in a jar

Take an empty jam jar and put in a drop of squeezy washing-up liquid. Then fill most of the jar with water but leave 2 cm for air at the top. Pour in some glitter.

Now put the lid on the jar and shake it round in a circular motion. You should see your very own mini tornado!

Tornado damage

Unlike a hurricane, a tornado is usually no more than half a kilometre wide at the ground. It travels at about 50 to 100 km/h and cuts a path of destruction through the landscape. Either side of this path is left undamaged. Some structures and vehicles can be sucked up and carried for a distance before being dropped back to Earth.

Damage caused by a tornado.

Heatwaves

A spell of much hotter than normal summer temperatures, lasting days or weeks, is called a heatwave. However, what would be considered a heatwave in a cool part of the world might be normal weather for a hotter area.

For example, people might talk about a heatwave in Britain if temperatures reach up to 30 °C for a time. In India, long spells of temperatures above 40 °C in plains and 30 °C in hills would be considered to be heatwaves.

High pressure

When there is high pressure air is pushed down towards the Earth and so clouds cannot form. Hot air is held in and temperatures can build higher and higher.

Many people enjoy hot weather, especially if they have fun ways to cool down.

A water sprinkler in the square, Krakow, Poland.

Health effects

During heatwaves the very young, elderly, or seriously ill are more vulnerable to health problems. They are at risk of not having enough water in their bodies, and of overheating. During heatwaves there can be 2000–3000 more deaths than normal. This happened during the 2015 Indian heatwave. The heat also caused power cuts and so air-conditioning systems failed.

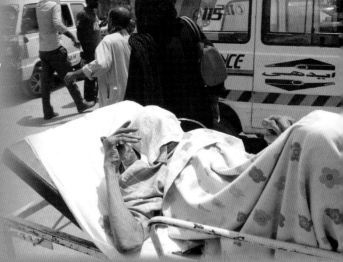

A heatstroke patient during a heatwave in Pakistan.

Wildfires

When crops and forests get very dry and there are hot winds blowing, there is a high risk of fires starting and getting out of control. These wildfires can cause massive destruction to the landscape and animal life, as well as to property.

Drought

During heatwaves there can be water shortages and droughts. Soil becomes baked and cracked and crops can fail if there is no water.

A bush fire burning at night in Australia.

47

Blizzards

Blizzards are very heavy snowstorms which come at the same time as chilling winds of over 56 km/h (35 mph). They last for at least 3 hours and some can go on for several days. The temperatures feel very cold because of the wind.

Poor visibility

During blizzards it can be hard to see further than a few hundred metres because of the wind-driven snow. This makes for very dangerous driving conditions.

A **whiteout** is when you cannot see further than a few metres and all is white around you. People can easily lose their sense of direction if out walking in a whiteout. It can be very dangerous to be on the hills in these conditions.

Cold winds in blizzards can quickly lead to people getting frostbite or hypothermia (a dangerous condition when body temperatures drop too low).

Snowdrifts

Huge piles of snow can build up due to snow drifting during blizzards. These are known as snowdrifts. They can block transport routes and hide walls and fences, causing difficulties on the road. Vehicles and buildings can be partly buried in them. They can even bury livestock out in the fields.

This is a stop sign at Winter Drive and Blizzard Street during a blizzard!

·············>

Ground blizzards

Sometimes high winds cause loose snow that has already fallen to be blown up from the ground to form snowdrifts in new places. This is called a ground blizzard and it creates low visibility.

A blizzard on the road and bad visibility in Hokkaido, Japan.

Luckily for drivers in the Rocky Mountains National Park, USA, this snowdrift has been ploughed through to keep the road clear.

Thunderstorms

Thunderstorms happen when large amounts of moisture in warm fast-rising air form huge towering clouds called cumulonimbus. Powerful electrical charges build up in these clouds and this is what causes thunder and lightning. Another name for a thunderstorm is an **electrical storm**.

Lightning

Ice particles bump into each other and cause electrical charges to build up in the cloud. Electric currents shoot between positively and negatively charged areas. This is what we see as lightning. Thunder is the noise of air vibrating as it suddenly heats up then cools very quickly during a lightning strike.

Try this!

Rub a balloon over your hair and then lift it slightly above your head. Your hair may stand on end! This is because you have created positive and negative electric charges, which make some **static electricity.**

Sometimes you can hear static electricity crackle when you take a woolly top off over your head.

Thunderclouds

'When mountains and cliffs in the sky appear, Some sudden and violent storms are near.'

G. Herbert

You cannot hear thunder over 10 miles away but you can see 'flash lightning' further away. Sometimes all you see is a flash of light coming from within a cloud.

How to tell how far away a storm is

Light travels through air faster than sound. When lightning strikes around 1.5 km (1 mile) away you hear thunder 5 seconds after seeing the lightning. So if you count the seconds between a lightning flash and hearing thunder then divide the number by 5, that is how far away the storm is. If you do not have time to count, take cover because the lightning is striking right above you!

Most lightning appears as forked lightning.

Did you know?

Most thunderstorms occur in afternoons or evenings. This is when the day's heat has built up and towering thunderclouds have made enough electric charge in them to produce lightning.

51

Monsoons

For some countries in tropical areas the hot dry summer season is followed by heavy monsoon rains. These bring heavy daily rain for several months and can cause severe flooding.

What causes monsoons?

During the summer months in the tropics the land gets warmer than the ocean. This causes air to rise over the land. The cooler air from the ocean blows onto the land, bringing with it lots of moisture to form monsoon clouds. These clouds then rise up and burst with heavy rainfall.

The result of monsoon rains in Varanasi, India.

Monsoon rain in Borneo.

Monsoon systems

The Indian summer monsoon lasts from June to September.

In North America the southwest part of the USA can be affected by heavy rains and storms from July to September.

There is a West African monsoon that can cause storms to cluster and blow over the Atlantic Ocean to become hurricanes.

Barron Falls, Australia, after heavy monsoon rains.

An Indian woman walks in a flooded street in Calcutta, India, 2015.

Asian-Australian monsoon

In the southern hemisphere the summer months of December to March bring monsoon weather to southeast Asia and northern Australia.

An unusually heavy monsoon flood in Ayuttaya, Thailand.

Effects of extreme weather

Extreme weather can kill people and destroys land and property. Damaged crops and loss of livestock mean people lose their livelihoods.

Hurricanes are most destructive when they hit land. Not only do the high winds cause damage, huge waves called 'storm surges' result in flooding over coastal areas.

Severe monsoon rains lead to terrible flooding and loss of life. Torrential rains can also create massive mudslides, which can destroy roads and property and even cause injury or death.

Heatwaves may be fun for some, but for others, especially in the poorest parts of the world, they cause thousands of deaths due to droughts and famines.

Flooded streets in York, UK, after heavy rain in December 2015.

This mudslide cut through a road in Manyara, Tanzania, after a bad storm in 2011.

Drought and famine

Heatwaves and extreme heat can lead to a drought. People who depend on rains to water their crops and feed their livestock suffer most when there is no rain year after year. Richer countries are better able to cope with drought, but for many poorer countries this leads to famine.

Preparing for extreme weather

Weather forecasters use aircraft, satellites, and supercomputers to help them give early warnings of extreme weather events. They are able to give more accurate predictions of 'what, where and when' than ever before. But even then the weather can suddenly change and cause surprises.

HURRICANE EVACUATION ROUTE

Evacuation plans

HURRICANE SHELTER

People who are used to extreme weather have plans put in place to help them stay as safe as possible. For some people it is by being prepared and knowing exactly where they will go in an emergency. People may have supplies kept in case of emergencies, like food, water, torches, spare batteries, a first aid kit, and changes of clothing. They may also have lists of emergency contact numbers.

Many people put out sandbags to protect their properties from flooding. Some schools practise drills, for example they may have a flood drill, where they evacuate to higher ground.

In some areas people have tornado or hurricane shelters built so that they have somewhere safe to go in the event of an emergency.

Sandbags piled up to stop flooding.

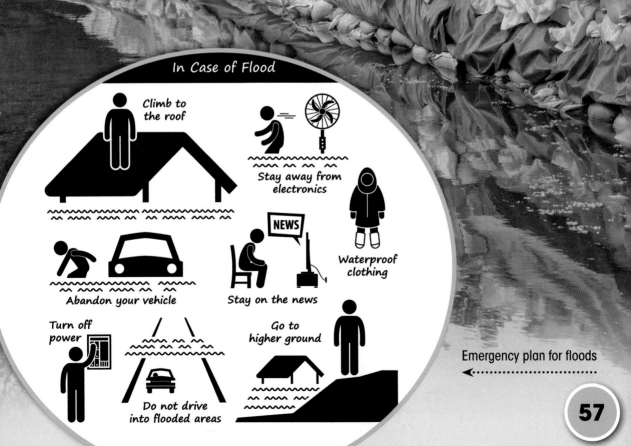

In Case of Flood

Climb to the roof

Stay away from electronics

Abandon your vehicle

Stay on the news

Waterproof clothing

Turn off power

Do not drive into flooded areas

Go to higher ground

Emergency plan for floods

World records

The World Meteorological Organization (WMO) has published records compiled from weather stations all over the world since 1927.

These records can be used to find out the hottest, coldest, wettest, driest, and windiest places on Earth.

On July 10, 1913, Death Valley measured a temperature of 56.7 °C, the hottest on record.

Hottest places

Ciudad Bolívar in Venezuela has temperatures above 34 °C every month of the year.

Coldest places

The Russian research station of Vostok, Antarctica, holds the record for the coldest ever temperatures recorded at a weather station: -89.2 °C

However a NASA satellite recorded a low of -93.2 °C near Dome Argus in Antarctica. This area has the lowest annual mean temperature of -58.3 °C.

The city of Yakutsk in Russia has the lowest winter temperatures of any city in the world. Its average winter temperature is -34 °C. A Yakutsk party trick is to throw a kettle of boiling water out of a window and watch it instantly blow away in a cloud!

Wettest and driest places

Meghalaya State in India is one of the wettest places on Earth, with its town of Mawsynram recording 11 872 mm (that is nearly 12 m) of rain a year.

◄ ···

The city of Arica in Chile, South America, is the driest city, with an average of 0.76 mm of rain a year. Between October 1903 and January 1918 there was no rainfall at all. That is nearly 14 years without rain!

◄ ·································

Windiest place

Barrow Island in Australia recorded the highest gust of wind at 408 km/h (253 mph). This was during tropical storm Olivia in April 1996. Port Martin in Antarctica is the windiest place in general as it has, at least, over 100 days a year when the winds blow at over 64 km/h (40 mph).

Weather and the world around us

Global warming

Climate change

Climate change and ecosystems

Global warming

Earth's atmosphere is made up of gases that help trap heat from the Sun, creating what scientists call the 'greenhouse effect'. It is called this because the atmosphere acts like the glass in a greenhouse. This is what gives Earth its temperature and climate. However, gases that trap heat in the atmosphere – so-called 'greenhouse gases' – have been building up over time and this is leading to increasing global temperatures. Scientists call this man-made global warming.

Greenhouse gases

The main greenhouse gas is **carbon dioxide**, CO_2. This is actually the gas that we breathe out. In the past century it has been produced in huge amounts from burning coal, oil, or petrol and diesel.

Car exhaust fumes also give off CO_2.

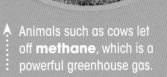
Animals such as cows let off **methane**, which is a powerful greenhouse gas.

Rainforest plants take in CO_2 from the air and give out oxygen. But the destruction of rainforests means less CO_2 is being naturally soaked up. In addition, if rainforests are cleared by burning, CO_2 is released in smoke.

Climate change

The climate of any region on Earth is its typical weather when it is measured over 30 years. For example, some places have hot dry climates, some areas have hot wet climates, and polar areas are cold and icy. Temperate zones are neither very hot nor very cold.

Climate change and global warming

Earth's climate has often varied. It has had periods of cooling which have led to Ice Ages, and warmer tropical periods. Climate change is nothing new, but it has taken place over thousands and millions of years. However, in the past century our planet has been warming up at a much faster rate. Scientists have taken measurements which show temperatures rising way above the normal expected range for the past century. This global warming is leading to rapid climate change which in turn is affecting the weather around the world

Scientists in the Arctic region are concerned at the rate at which the Arctic Ocean's cap of ice is melting. Ice-free channels are opening up routes for shipping which were once impassable. Wildlife is being threatened by loss of habitat.

More extreme weather

Scientists are predicting that global warming will lead to more extremes of weather such as heatwaves and droughts in some areas. Other areas may have much heavier rain or snowfall. More flooding is expected not only from storms but also from increasing sea levels as the ice caps melt.

Effects on ocean currents

As polar ice caps melt and cold icy water enters the oceans it could be that the ocean currents completely change. Parts of the world used to mild ocean climates could become much colder instead of warmer.

Most scientists agree that global warming and climate change are taking place, and there is a lot of research being done to understand what and where the effects might be.

How people would cope with climate change would vary, probably depending on how different societies would be able to adapt and prepare for changes.

Climate change and ecosystems

Land and oceans influence weather systems but weather affects what grows and lives in the environment. Changes in one system lead to changes in the other.

The rainforest

Rainforest vegetation is adapted to hot tropical temperatures and daily rainfall. Plants and animals depend on these conditions.

However, the rainforest is being destroyed at an alarming rate and many animals and plants are becoming extinct. Not only that, but the loss of forest is leading to global warming, which is changing our planet's weather patterns.

Coral reefs

Coral reefs are found in tropical oceans near the Equator. The largest and perhaps best known one is the Great Barrier Reef off the east coast of Australia. Coral reefs are colourful underwater 'mini forests' with huge varieties of plants and fishes.

A rise in ocean temperature of just 1 °C can lead to 'bleaching', which means colourful algae leave the coral and it then turns white. If warmer conditions continue, the algae stay away and the coral cannot recover from this state.

Global warming is a very real threat to coral reefs.

A healthy coral reef and a bleached coral reef.

Tundra regions

Tundra extends over one-fifth of the land on Earth and is found in cold polar regions. There are hardly any trees there and much of the ground is frozen all year round, which makes 'permafrost'. Warmer temperatures threaten the environment on which animals and plants depend. One animal under threat is the polar bear.

Looking after the ecosystem

People realise that their industries and modern developments are harming Earth's climate and that weather patterns seem to be changing. Now humans are learning to harness the power of weather to make more 'eco-friendly' or 'greener' energy. For example, wind farms on land and at sea can make electricity instead of burning coal and gas. We can also make use of sunshine by using solar panels to capture and make energy.

Useful words

altitude   The height of something above sea level.

arc   A smoothly curving line.

atmosphere   The air and other gases that surround a planet.

avalanche   A huge mass of snow and ice that falls down a mountainside.

°C , Celsius   A scale for measuring temperature in which water freezes at 0 degrees (0 °C) and boils at 100 degrees (100 °C). It is named after Anders Celsius (1701–1744), who invented it.

Centigrade   Means the same as Celsius.

climate   The typical weather conditions in a place.

condense   When a gas or vapour changes into a liquid.

continent   A very large area of land such as Africa, Europe, or Asia.

contour   A line on a map joining points of equal height above sea level.

coral   A hard substance that forms in the sea from the skeletons of tiny animals called corals.

crystal   A piece of a mineral that has formed naturally into a regular shape.

drought   A long period during which there is no rain.

ecosystem   The relationship between plants and animals and their environment.

electrical charge   The amount of electricity that something carries.

emission   The release of something such as a gas or radiation into the atmosphere.

Equator   An imaginary line drawn round the middle of the Earth, lying half way between the North and South Poles.

evaporate   When a liquid becomes less and less as it changes into a gas.

°F , Fahrenheit   A scale of temperature in which the freezing point of water is 32 °F and the boiling point is 212 °F.

famine A serious shortage of food which may cause many deaths.

gauge A piece of equipment that measures the amount of something.

hemisphere One half of the Earth.

isobar A line on a map which joins places of equal air pressure.

latitude The distance of a place north or south of the Equator measured in degrees.

millibar A unit of atmospheric pressure equal to one thousandth of a bar.

moisture Tiny drops of water in the air or on the ground.

particle A very small piece of something.

pressure The force that is produced by pushing on something.

prism An object made of clear glass with many flat sides. It separates light passing through it into the colours of the rainbow.

radiation The stream of powerful and harmful rays from a radioactive substance.

satellite A spacecraft sent into orbit around the Earth to collect information.

spectrum The range of different colours produced when light passes through a prism or a drop of water.

temperate Having weather that is neither extremely hot nor extremely cold.

tropics The hottest part of the world between two lines of latitude, the Tropic of Cancer, 23.5 degrees north of the Equator and the Tropic of Capricorn, 23.5 degrees south of the Equator.

tundra A vast treeless Arctic region.

vapour A mass of tiny drops of water or other liquids in the air which looks like mist.

wavelength The length of a wave from one wave tip to the next.

Index

Acknowledgements

Publisher: Anne Mahon
Project Manager: Craig Balfour
Designer: Kevin Robbins
Layout: Craig Balfour
Text: Sarah Thurlbeck
Editorial: Maree Airlee, Jill Laidlaw, Louise Robb

Photo credits

Cover image
Tornado: sdecoret/Shutterstock.com
Leaves: LilKar/Shutterstock.com
Glacier: meunierd/Shutterstock.com

t=top, c=centre, b=bottom, l=left, r=right   SS=Shutterstock

p2-3, solarseven/SS; **p4-5** Minerva Studio/SS; **p4** Christian Mueller/SS (t); iyd39/SS (b); **p5** Igor Zh/SS; **p6-7** Pakhnyushchy/SS; **p8-9** studio23/SS; **p8** hkeita/SS; **p9** Designua/SS; **p10-11** alybaba/SS; **p10** OlegDoroshin/SS; **p11** Gabriele Maltinti/SS/SS (t); Mimadeo/SS (c); Martchan/SS (b); **p12** Maksym Darakchi/SS; **p13** RossHelen/SS (t); artjazz/SS (l); blackpixel/SS (r); Danette C/SS (b); **p14-15** patpitchaya/SS; **p14** FamVeld/SS (t); Merkushev Vasiliy/SS (b); **p15** Nuttapong Wongcheronkit/SS (l); Webspark/SS (r) **p16-17** Pakhnyushchy/SS; **p16** Twin Design/SS (t); **p17** Jason Batterham/SS (t); Songchai W/SS (b); **p18-19** Brian A Jackson/SS; **p18** Jamilia Marini/SS; **p19** Sander van der Werf/SS (t); Nickolay Vinokurov/SS (c); aragami12345s/SS (b); **p20-21** my nordic/SS; **p20** Kichigin/SS (l); Kichigin/SS (c); Kichigin/SS (r); **p21** Sergey Pesterev/SS (t); Alex Egorov/SS (b); **p22-23** Pyty/SS; **p22** Olga Gavrilova/SS (t); Sarah Thurlbeck (l); Ewan Chesser/SS (r); **p23** meunierd/SS (t); Denis Burdin/SS (b); **p24-25** erapictures/SS; **p26-27** Redsapphire/SS; **p27** ffoto/SS (t); Konrad Mostert/SS (l); Silberkorn/SS (r); **p28-29** Patrick Jennings/SS; **p28** ChameleonsEye/SS; **p29** Sarah Thurlbeck; **P30-31** OlegDoroshin/SS; **p30** Flipser/SS; **p31** flaviano fabrizi/SS (t); Sarah Thurlbeck (b); **p32** f-f-f-f/SS (t); AlexLMX/SS (c); EggHeadPhoto (b); **p33** Sarah Thurlbeck; **p34** Robert Adrian Hillman/SS (t); NgFotografia/SS (b) ; **p35** Robert Adrian Hillman/SS (t); Frank Fiedler/SS (c); UMB-O/SS (b); **p36-37** karrapavan/SS; **p36** Fineart1/SS (t); gyn9037/SS (l); Marafona/SS (r); **p37** Sunny Celeste/SS; **p38-39** Walid Nohra/SS; **p38** UMB-O/SS (t); antb/SS (b); **p39** Six Dun/SS (t); Evlakhov Valeriy/SS (b); **p40-41** solarseven/SS; **p42** Harvepino /SS (t); MISHELLA/SS (b); **p43** zstock/SS (t); Niar/SS (c); Pattie Steib/SS (b); **p44-45** Minerva Studio/SS; **p45** Rob Byron/SS (t); Alexey Stiop/SS (b); **p46** ChameleonsEye/SS (t); praszkiewicz/SS (b); **p47** Asianet-Pakistan/SS (t); VanderWolf Images/SS (c); John Kasawa/SS (b); **p48** Jan Mika/SS (t); Mikadun/SS (b); **p49** Phil McDonald/SS (t); arongsak Nagadhana/(c); Sopotnicki/SS (b); **p50-51** Vasin Lee/SS; **p50** Rustam Shanov/SS; **p51** Creative Travel Projects/SS (t); aapsky/SS (b); **p52** c. mokri - austria/SS (t); Daniel J. Rao/SS (b); **p53** Saikat Paul/SS (t); Wendy Townrow/SS (c); Thor Jorgen Udvang/SS (b); **p54** Photobank gallery/SS; **p55** Phil MacD Photography/SS (t); Vadim Petrakov/SS (c); Earl D. Walker/SS (b); **p56** rnl/SS (t); RHIMAGE/SS (b); **p57** serato/SS (t); Leremy/SS (b); **p58-59** Nagel Photography/SS; **p58** gary yim/SS; **p59** Public domain (t); Daniel J. Rao /ss (l); JeremyRichards/SS (r); **p60-61** moomsabuy/SS; **p62** daulon/ss; **p63** Mikael Damkier/SS (t); Ungnoi Lookjeab/SS (l); Dudarev Mikhail/SS (r); Robin Kay/SS (b); **p64** koya979/SS (t); Jan Martin Will (b); **p65** Sam72/SS (t); Piyaset/SS (b); **p66** Vlad61/SS (t); Kozoriz Yuriy/SS (l); Ethan Daniels/SS (r); **p67** Sergey Uryadnikov/SS (t); Smileus/SS (c); Stephen Bures/SS (b); **p68-69** Kirill Smirnov/SS; **p70-71** Amirul Abdul Razak/SS, **p72** Mimadeo/SS